D0665981

Key Element Guide
ITIL® Service Operation

London: TSO

information & publishing solutions

Published by TSO (The Stationery Office) and
available from:

Online
www.tsoshop.co.uk

Mail, Telephone, Fax & E-mail
TSO
PO Box 29, Norwich, NR3 1GN
Telephone orders/General enquiries:
0870 600 5522
Fax orders: 0870 600 5533
E-mail: customer.services@tso.co.uk
Textphone 0870 240 3701

TSO@Blackwell and other Accredited Agents

First edition Crown copyright 2008
Second edition Crown copyright 2012

Third impression 2014

ISBN 9780113313631 (Single copy ISBN)
ISBN 9780113313686 (Sold in a pack of 10
copies)

Printed in the United Kingdom for The
Stationery Office

Material is FSC certified and produced using
ECF pulp, sourced from fully sustainable forests.

P002500757   c18   07/12

Contents

Acknowledgements

AUTHOR

Randy Steinberg, Migration Technologies Inc.

KEY ELEMENT GUIDE AUTHORING TEAM

David Cannon, BMC Software

Ashley Hanna, HP

Lou Hunnebeck, Third Sky Inc.

Vernon Lloyd, Fox IT

Stuart Rance, HP

REVIEWERS

Best Management Practice and The Stationery Office would like to thank itSMF International for managing the quality assurance of this publication, and the following reviewers for their contributions:

Duncan Anderson, Global Knowledge; John Donoghue, Allied Irish Bank plc; John Earle, itSMF Ireland Ltd; Robert Falkowitz, Concentric Circle Consulting; Padraig Farrell, SureSkills; Siobhan Flaherty, Generali PanEurope; Signe Marie Hernes Bjerke, Det Norske Veritas; Michael Imhoff Nielsen, IBM; Jackie Manning, Bord Gáis Networks; Krikor Maroukian, King's College London; Reiko Morita, Ability InterBusiness Solutions, Inc.; Trevor Murray, The Grey Matters; Gary O'Dwyer, Allied Irish Banks plc; Benjamin Orazem, SRC d.o.o.; Sue Shaw, TriCentrica; Marco Smith, iCore Ltd; Hon P Suen, ECT Service Ltd; and Paul Wigzel, Paul Wigzel Training and Consultancy.

1 Introduction

This key element guide is intended to provide a summary of the basic concepts and practice elements of *ITIL Service Operation*, which forms part of the core ITIL publication suite.

ITIL is a set of best-practice publications for IT service management (ITSM).[1] ITIL provides guidance on the provision of quality IT services, and on the capabilities needed to support them. ITIL is not a standard that has to be followed; it is guidance that should be read and understood, and used to create value for the service provider and its customers. Organizations are encouraged to adopt ITIL best practices and to adapt them to work in their specific environments in ways that meet their needs.

ITIL is the most widely recognized framework for ITSM in the world. In the 20 years since it was created, ITIL has evolved and changed its breadth and depth as technologies and business practices have developed.

The section numbering in this key element guide is not the same as the section numbers in the core publication, *ITIL Service Operation*. Therefore, do not try to use references to section numbers in the core publication when referencing material in this key element guide.

1.1 THE ITIL SERVICE LIFECYCLE

The ITIL framework is based on five stages of the service lifecycle as shown in Figure 1.1, with a core publication providing

---

[1] ITSM and other concepts from this chapter are described in more detail in Chapter 2.

Figure 1.1 The ITIL service lifecycle

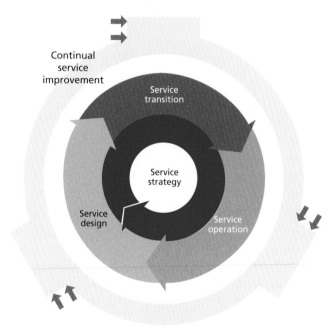

best-practice guidance for each stage. This guidance includes principles, processes and activities, organization and roles, technology, challenges, critical success factors, and risks. The service lifecycle uses a hub-and-spoke design, with service strategy at the hub, and service design, service transition and service operation as the revolving lifecycle stages or 'spokes'.

Continual service improvement surrounds and supports all stages of the service lifecycle. Each stage of the lifecycle exerts influence on the others and relies on them for inputs and feedback. In this way, a constant set of checks and balances ensures that as business demand changes, the services can adapt and respond effectively.

In addition to the core publications, there is also a complementary set of ITIL publications providing guidance specific to industry sectors, organization types, operating models and technology architectures.

The following key characteristics of ITIL contribute to its global success:

- **Vendor-neutral** ITIL service management practices are not based on any particular technology platform or industry type. ITIL is owned by the UK government and is not tied to any commercial proprietary practice or solution.
- **Non-prescriptive** ITIL offers robust, mature and time-tested practices that have applicability to all types of service organization. It continues to be useful and relevant in public and private sectors, internal and external service providers, small, medium and large enterprises, and within any technical environment.
- **Best practice** ITIL represents the learning experiences and thought leadership of the world's best-in-class service providers.

1.2   SERVICE OPERATION – KEY ELEMENT GUIDE

ITIL Service Operation provides best-practice guidance for the service operation stage of the service lifecycle.

1.2.1   Purpose and objectives of service operation

The purpose of service operation is to coordinate and carry out the activities and processes required to deliver and manage services to business users and customers at agreed levels. Service operation is also responsible for the ongoing management of the technology that is used to deliver and support services.

The objectives of service operation are to:

- Maintain business satisfaction and confidence in IT through effective and efficient delivery and support of agreed IT services
- Minimize the impact of service outages on day-to-day business activities
- Ensure that access to agreed IT services is only provided to those authorized to receive those services.

1.2.2   Scope

ITIL Service Operation describes the processes, functions, organization and tools used to underpin the ongoing activities required to deliver and support services. The guidance provided in the core publication includes:

- **The services themselves** Activities that form part of a service are included in service operation, whether it is performed by the service provider, an external supplier or the user or customer of that service.
- **Service management processes** The ongoing management and execution of the many service management processes that are performed in service operation. Even though a number of ITIL processes originate at other stages of the service lifecycle, they are in use continually in service operation.

- **Technology** A large part of *ITIL Service Operation* is concerned with the management of the infrastructure used to deliver services.
- **People** Regardless of what services, processes and technology are managed, they are all about people. Failure to recognize this will result in the failure of service management activities.

1.2.3 Value to business

Adopting and implementing standard and consistent approaches for service operation will:

- Reduce unplanned labour and costs for both the business and IT through optimized handling of service outages and identification of their root causes.
- Reduce the duration and frequency of service outages, which will allow the business to take full advantage of the value created by the services they are receiving.
- Provide operational results and data that can be used by other ITIL processes to improve services continually and provide justification for investing in ongoing service improvement activities and supporting technologies.
- Meet the goals and objectives of the organization's security policy by ensuring that IT services will be accessed only by those authorized to use them.
- Provide quick and effective access to standard services which business staff can use to improve their productivity or the quality of business services and products.
- Provide a basis for automated operations, thus increasing efficiencies and allowing expensive human resources to be used for more innovative work.

1.3   CONTEXT

Each core ITIL publication addresses those capabilities that have a direct impact on a service provider's performance. The core is expected to provide structure, stability and strength to service management capabilities, with durable principles, methods and tools. This serves to protect investments and provide the necessary basis for measurement, learning and improvement.

1.3.1   Service strategy

At the centre of the service lifecycle is service strategy. Value creation begins here with understanding organizational objectives and customer needs. Every organizational asset, including people, processes and products, should support the strategy.

ITIL Service Strategy provides guidance on how to view service management not only as an organizational capability but as a strategic asset. It describes the principles underpinning the practice of service management which are useful for developing service management policies, guidelines and processes across the service lifecycle.

Organizations already practising ITIL can use *ITIL Service Strategy* to guide a strategic review of their service management capabilities and to improve the alignment between those capabilities and their business strategies. *ITIL Service Strategy* will encourage readers to stop and think about *why* something is to be done before thinking of *how*.

1.3.2   Service design

Service design is the stage in the lifecycle that turns a service strategy into a plan for delivering business objectives. *ITIL Service*

Design provides guidance for the design and development of services and service management practices. It covers design principles and methods for converting strategic objectives into portfolios of services and service assets. The scope of *ITIL Service Design* includes the changes and improvements necessary to increase or maintain value to customers over the lifecycle of services, the continuity of services, the achievement of service levels, and conformance to standards and regulations.

1.3.3   Service transition

ITIL Service Transition provides guidance for the development and improvement of capabilities for introducing new and changed services into supported environments. It describes how to transition an organization from one state to another while controlling risk and supporting organizational knowledge for decision support. It ensures that the value(s) identified in the service strategy, and encoded in the service design, are effectively transitioned so that they can be realized in service operation.

1.3.4   Service operation

ITIL Service Operation describes best practice for managing services in supported environments. It includes guidance on achieving effectiveness and efficiency in the delivery and support of services to ensure value for the customer, the users and the service provider. *ITIL Service Operation* provides guidance on how to maintain stability in service operation, even while allowing for changes in design, scale, scope and service levels.

1.3.5   Continual service improvement

ITIL Continual Service Improvement provides guidance on creating and maintaining value for customers through better strategy, design, transition and operation of services. It combines principles, practices and methods from quality management, change management and capability improvement.

ITIL Continual Service Improvement describes best practice for achieving incremental and large-scale improvements in service quality, operational efficiency and business continuity, and for ensuring that the service portfolio continues to be aligned to business needs.

2 Service management as a practice

2.1 SERVICES AND SERVICE MANAGEMENT

2.1.1 Services

Definitions

Service: A means of delivering value to customers by facilitating outcomes customers want to achieve without the ownership of specific costs and risks.

IT service: A service provided by an IT service provider. An IT service is made up of a combination of information technology, people and processes. A customer-facing IT service directly supports the business processes of one or more customers and its service level targets should be defined in a service level agreement. Other IT services, called supporting services, are not directly used by the business but are required by the service provider to deliver customer-facing services.

Outcome: The result of carrying out an activity, following a process, or delivering an IT service etc. The term is used to refer to intended results, as well as to actual results.

An outcome-based definition of service moves IT organizations beyond business–IT alignment towards business–IT integration. Customers seek outcomes but do not wish to have accountability or ownership of all the associated costs and risks. The customer can judge the value of a service based on a comparison of cost or price and reliability with the desired outcome. Customer satisfaction is also important. Customer expectations keep shifting, and a service provider that does not track this will soon lose business.

2.1.2   Service management

Business would like IT services to behave like other utilities such as water, electricity or the telephone. Simply having the best technology does not ensure that the IT service will provide utility-like reliability. Service management can bring this utility quality of service to the business.

> **Definitions**
>
> *Service management*: A set of specialized organizational capabilities for providing value to customers in the form of services.
>
> *Service provider*: An organization supplying services to one or more internal or external customers.

The more mature a service provider's capabilities are, the greater is their ability to meet the needs of the customer. The act of transforming capabilities and resources into valuable services is at the core of service management. The origins of service management are in traditional service businesses such as airlines, banks and hotels.

2.1.3   IT service management

Every IT organization should act as a service provider, using service management to ensure that they deliver outcomes required by their customers. A service level agreement (SLA) is used to document agreements between an IT service provider and a customer. An SLA describes the service, documents targets, and specifies the responsibilities of the service provider and the customer.

2.1.4   Service providers

There are three main types of service provider:

- **Type I – internal service provider** This type is embedded within a business unit. There may be several Type I service providers within an organization.
- **Type II – shared services unit** An internal service provider that provides shared IT services to more than one business unit.
- **Type III – external service provider** A service provider that provides IT services to external customers.

IT service management (ITSM) concepts are often described in the context of only one of these types. In reality most organizations have a combination of IT service provider types.

2.1.5   Stakeholders in service management

Stakeholders have an interest in an organization, project or service etc. and may also be interested in the activities, targets, resources or deliverables. There are many stakeholders inside the service provider. There are also many external stakeholders, for example:

- **Customers** Those who buy goods or services. Customers define and agree the service level targets.
- **Users** Those who use the service on a day-to-day basis.
- **Suppliers** Third parties responsible for supplying goods or services that are required to deliver IT services.

There is a difference between internal customers and external customers:

- **Internal customers** These work for the same business as the service provider – for example, the marketing department uses IT services.
- **External customers** These work for a different business from the service provider. External customers typically purchase services by means of a legally binding contract or agreement.

2.1.6   Utility and warranty

From the customer's perspective, value consists of achieving business objectives. The value of a service is created by combining utility (fitness for purpose) and warranty (fitness for use).

- **Utility** is the ability to meet a particular need. It is often described as 'what the service does' – for example, a service that enables a business unit to process orders.
- **Warranty** is an assurance that the service will meet its agreed requirements. Warranty includes the ability of a service to be available when needed, to provide the required capacity, and to provide the required reliability in terms of continuity and security.

The value of a service is only created when both utility and warranty are designed and delivered.

Information about the desired business outcomes, opportunities, customers, utility and warranty of the service is used to develop the definition of a service. Using an outcome-based definition helps to ensure that managers plan and execute all aspects of service management from the customer's perspective.

2.1.7 Best practices in the public domain

Organizations benchmark themselves against peers and seek to close gaps in capabilities. This enables them to become more competitive. One way to close gaps is the adoption of best practices. There are several sources for best practice including public frameworks, standards and the proprietary knowledge of organizations and individuals. ITIL is the most widely recognized and trusted source of best-practice guidance for ITSM.

2.2 BASIC CONCEPTS

2.2.1 Assets, resources and capabilities

The relationship between service providers and customers revolves around the use of assets – both those of the service provider and those of the customer. The performance of customer assets is a primary concern for service management.

> **Definitions**
>
> *Asset*: Any resource or capability.
>
> *Customer asset*: Any resource or capability used by a customer to achieve a business outcome.
>
> *Service asset*: Any resource or capability used by a service provider to deliver services to a customer.

There are two types of asset – resources and capabilities. Resources are direct inputs for production. Capabilities represent an organization's ability to coordinate, control and deploy resources to produce value. It is relatively easy to acquire resources compared to capabilities. Figure 2.1 shows examples of capabilities and resources.

Figure 2.1 Examples of capabilities and resources

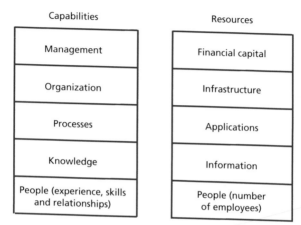

2.2.2   Processes

Definition: process

A process is a structured set of activities designed to accomplish a specific objective. A process takes one or more defined inputs and turns them into defined outputs.

Process characteristics include:

- **Measurability** We can measure the process in a relevant manner.
- **Specific results** The process delivers specific results, which must be individually identifiable and countable.

■ **Customers** The process delivers its primary results to a customer or stakeholder. Customers may be internal or external to the organization.
■ **Responsiveness to specific triggers** The process should be traceable to a specific trigger.

The outputs from the process should be driven by the process objectives. Process measurement and metrics can be built into the process to control and improve the process as illustrated in Figure 2.2.

Figure 2.2 Process model

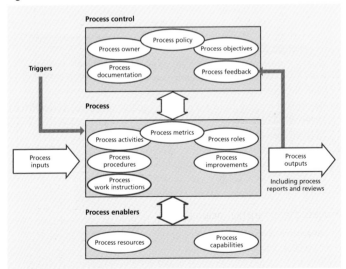

2.2.3   Organizing for service management

Best practices described in ITIL need to be tailored to suit organizations and situations. The starting point for organizational design is service strategy.

2.2.3.1   Functions

A function is a team or group of people and the tools or other resources they use to carry out one or more processes or activities. In larger organizations, a function may be performed by several departments, teams and groups. In smaller organizations, one person or group can perform multiple functions – for example, a technical management department could also incorporate the service desk function.

ITIL Service Operation describes the following functions:

- **Service desk** The single point of contact for users. A typical service desk manages incidents and service requests, and also handles communication with the users.
- **Technical management** Provides technical skills and resources needed to manage the IT infrastructure throughout the service lifecycle.
- **IT operations management** Executes the daily operational activities needed to manage IT services and the supporting IT infrastructure.
- **Application management** Is responsible for managing applications throughout their lifecycle. This differs from application development which is mainly concerned with one-time activities for requirements, design and build of applications.

The other core ITIL publications rely on the technical and application management functions described in *ITIL Service Operation*, but they do not define any additional functions in detail.

2.2.3.2   Roles

The core ITIL publications provide guidelines and examples of role descriptions. In many cases roles will need to be combined or separated.

> **Definition: role**
>
> A role is a set of responsibilities, activities and authorities granted to a person or team. A role is defined in a process or function. One person or team may have multiple roles – for example, the roles of configuration manager and change manager may be carried out by a single person.

Roles are often confused with job titles but they are not the same. Each organization defines job titles and job descriptions, and individuals holding these job titles can perform one or more roles. See Chapter 5 for more details about roles and responsibilities.

2.2.4   The service portfolio

The service portfolio is the complete set of services managed by a service provider, and it represents the service provider's commitments and investments across all customers and market spaces. It consists of three parts:

- **Service pipeline** Services that are under consideration or development, but are not yet available to customers. The service pipeline is a service provider's business view of possible future services.
- **Service catalogue** Live IT services, including those available for deployment. It is the only part of the service portfolio that is published to customers. It includes a customer-facing view (or views) of the IT services. It also includes information about supporting services required by the service provider.
- **Retired services** Services that have retired.

Service providers often find it useful to distinguish customer-facing services from supporting services:

- **Customer-facing services** Visible to the customer. These normally support the customer's business processes and facilitate outcomes desired by the customer.
- **Supporting services** Support or 'underpin' the customer-facing services. These are typically invisible to the customer, but are essential to the delivery of customer-facing services.

Figure 2.3 illustrates the components of the service portfolio. These are important components of the service knowledge management system (SKMS) described in section 2.2.5.

2.2.5 Knowledge management and the SKMS

Knowledge and information enable people to perform activities and support information flow between lifecycle stages and processes. Implementing knowledge management enables effective decision support and reduces risks.

ITIL Service Transition describes an architecture for a service knowledge management system (SKMS) with four layers:

Figure 2.3 The service portfolio and its contents

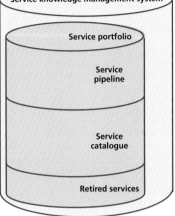

- **Presentation layer** Enables searching, browsing, retrieving, updating, subscribing and collaboration. Different views are provided for different audiences.
- **Knowledge-processing layer** Where information is converted into knowledge which enables decision-making.
- **Information integration layer** Provides integrated information from data in multiple sources in the data layer.
- **Data layer** Includes tools for data discovery and collection, and data items in unstructured and structured forms.

2.3   GOVERNANCE AND MANAGEMENT SYSTEMS

2.3.1   Governance

Governance defines the common directions, policies and rules that both the business and IT use to conduct business.

> **Definition: governance**
>
> Ensures that policies and strategy are actually implemented, and that required processes are correctly followed. Governance includes defining roles and responsibilities, measuring and reporting, and taking actions to resolve any issues identified.

Governance applies a consistently managed approach at all levels of the organization by ensuring a clear strategy is set, and by defining the policies needed to achieve the strategy.

2.3.2   Management systems

Many businesses have adopted management system standards for competitive advantage, to ensure a consistent approach in implementing service management, and to support governance.

An organization can adopt multiple management system standards, such as:

- A quality management system (ISO 9001)
- An environmental management system (ISO 14000)
- A service management system (ISO/IEC 20000)
- An information security management system (ISO/IEC 27001)
- A management system for software asset management (ISO/IEC 19770).

As there are common elements between such management systems, they should be managed in an integrated way rather than having separate management systems.

ISO management system standards use the Plan-Do-Check-Act (PDCA) cycle shown in Figure 2.4. This PDCA cycle is used in each of the core ITIL publications.

Figure 2.4 Plan-Do-Check-Act cycle

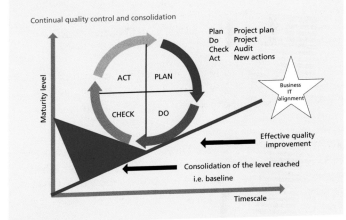

Definition: ISO/IEC 20000

An international standard for IT service management.

ISO/IEC 20000 is an international standard that allows organizations to prove best practice in ITSM. Part 1 specifies requirements for the service provider to plan, establish, implement, operate, monitor, review, maintain and improve a service management system (SMS). One of the most common routes for an organization to achieve the requirements of ISO/IEC 20000 is by adopting ITIL.

2.4 THE SERVICE LIFECYCLE

The service lifecycle is an organizing framework, supported by the organizational structure, service portfolio and service models within an organization. See Chapter 1 for an introduction to each ITIL service lifecycle stage.

2.4.1 Specialization and coordination across the lifecycle

Organizations should function in the same manner as a high-performing sports team. Each player in a team and each member of the team's organization who are not players position themselves to support the goal of the team. Each player and team member has a different specialization that contributes to the whole. The team matures over time taking into account feedback from experience, best practice and current processes and procedures to become an agile high-performing team.

Specialization allows for expert focus on components of the service but components of the service also need to work together for value. Coordination across the lifecycle creates an environment focused on business and customer outcomes instead of just IT objectives and projects. Specialization combined with coordination helps to manage expertise, improve focus and reduce overlaps and gaps in processes.

Adopting technology to automate the processes and provide management information that supports the processes is also important for effective and efficient service management.

2.4.2 Processes through the service lifecycle

Each core ITIL publication includes guidance on service
management processes as shown in Table 2.1.

Table 2.1 The processes described in each core ITIL publication

Core ITIL lifecycle publication	Processes described in the publication
ITIL Service Strategy	Strategy management for IT services Service portfolio management Financial management for IT services Demand management Business relationship management
ITIL Service Design	Design coordination Service catalogue management Service level management Availability management Capacity management IT service continuity management Information security management Supplier management

Table continues

Table 2.1 *continued*

Core ITIL lifecycle publication	Processes described in the publication
ITIL Service Transition	Transition planning and support Change management Service asset and configuration management Release and deployment management Service validation and testing Change evaluation Knowledge management
ITIL Service Operation	Event management Incident management Request fulfilment Problem management Access management
ITIL Continual Service Improvement	Seven-step improvement process

Most ITIL roles, processes and functions have activities that take place across multiple stages of the service lifecycle. For example:

■ Service validation and testing may design tests during the service design stage and perform these tests during service transition

■ Technical management provides input to strategic decisions about technology, and assists in the design and transition of infrastructure

■ Business relationship managers assist in gathering requirements during the service design stage of the lifecycle, and take part in the management of major incidents during the service operation stage.

The strength of the service lifecycle relies on continual feedback throughout each stage of the lifecycle. At every point in the service lifecycle, monitoring, assessment and feedback drives decisions about the need for minor course corrections or major service improvement initiatives.

3   Service operation principles

Service operation is responsible for:

- Executing and performing processes that optimize the cost and quality of services
- Enabling the business to meet its objectives
- Execution of operation control activities to manage and deliver services
- Delivering services within prescribed service levels
- Effective functioning of components that support services
- Maintaining user satisfaction with IT services.

It is through the service operation lifecycle stage that the business directly sees and receives value from its IT investments. This requires service operation practitioners to achieve a balance that focuses on effectively managing the day-to-day aspects while maintaining a perspective of the greater context.

3.1   SERVICE OPERATION FUNDAMENTALS

3.1.1   Providing business value through service operation

From a customer viewpoint, service operation is where actual value is seen. To achieve business value, service operation cannot solely focus on the internal aspects of day-to-day operation of services. An external view must also be taken that includes:

- Maintaining an understanding of the importance and impact of services on the business
- Providing clear metrics to the business on the achievement of service objectives, and reporting to IT managers on the efficiency and effectiveness of service operation

- Ensuring that all IT operations staff understand exactly how the performance of the technology affects the delivery of IT services and in turn how these affect the business and the business goals
- Ensuring involvement of IT operations staff in the service design and service transition stages of the service lifecycle
- Providing input from and feedback to continual service improvement (CSI) to identify areas that are out of balance and the means to identify and enforce improvement.

3.2   ACHIEVING BALANCE IN SERVICE OPERATION

All functions, processes and activities are designed to deliver specified and agreed levels of service, but they have to be delivered in an ever-changing environment. This forms a conflict between maintaining the status quo and adapting to changes in the business and technological environments. Service operation must deal with this conflict and achieve a balance between conflicting sets of priorities:

- **Internal IT view versus external business view** Service operation needs to balance the focus on business requirements versus thinking about how they will be delivered to avoid ending up with promises that cannot be kept. Conversely, a focus on internal systems without considering the services they support can result in expensive services that deliver little value.
- **Stability versus responsiveness** Service operation should ensure that the IT infrastructure is stable and available, yet also recognize that business and IT requirements change.
- **Quality of service versus cost of service** Service operation must balance the focus on quality versus cost, to avoid ending up with IT services that deliver more than necessary at higher

costs. Conversely, too much focus on cost will result in IT delivering within budget, but may put the business at risk through substandard IT services.

- **Reactive versus proactive** Service operation should avoid putting too much emphasis on responding to business requests and incidents only after they are reported. Conversely, IT may be too proactive, which may create higher than necessary costs and result in staff being distracted.

3.3   PROVIDING GOOD SERVICE

Equal emphasis should be placed on developing competencies to deal with customer relationships and interactions as well as technical competencies for managing the IT environment. For example, staff who deliver effective service may still cause significant customer dissatisfaction if they are insensitive or dismissive. Conversely, good customer relationships will not solve the problem if the service is not being delivered.

3.4   OPERATION STAFF INVOLVEMENT IN OTHER SERVICE LIFECYCLE STAGES

It is extremely important for service operation staff to be involved in activities taking place in other service lifecycle stages as follows:

- **Service strategy** To ensure that operational risks for IT strategies have been identified, gather and identify IT operational costs, and communicate current operation capabilities.
- **Service design** To ensure that what is designed can also be operated by defining operational requirements, linking

service specifications with performance of the IT infrastructure and mapping services with their underpinning technologies.

■ **Service transition** To ensure that stated business and manageability requirements are met by participating in operational acceptance tests, transitioning applications and components to the live environment, or validating operational readiness of a new service or major change.

■ **Continual service improvement** By identifying improvement opportunities for inclusion in the CSI register, promoting operational issues, providing operational data, and assessing the impact of proposed improvements on existing operation activities.

3.5   OPERATIONAL HEALTH

Operational health is determined by isolating important 'vital signs' on devices or services that are deemed critical for the successful execution of a vital business function. This could be bandwidth utilization on a network segment or memory utilization on a major server. If these signs are within normal ranges, the system is healthy and does not require additional attention.

Operational health is dependent on the ability to prevent incidents and problems by investing in reliable and maintainable infrastructure. This is achieved through good availability design and proactive problem management.

3.6   COMMUNICATION

Good communication is needed with other IT teams, users, internal customers, service operation teams and departments.

All communication must have an intended purpose. Information should not be communicated unless there is a clear audience. The audience should be actively involved in determining the need for that communication and what they will do with the information. There should be a review of communications on a periodic basis to validate that they are still required by the audience.

Examples of communication can include:

- Routine operational communication
- Communication between shifts
- Performance reporting
- Training on new or customized processes
- Communication of strategy, design and transition to service operation teams.

3.7   DOCUMENTATION

Service operation staff create and maintain documents that are stored in the service knowledge management system (SKMS). Activities include participation in the definition and maintenance of process manuals, establishing technical procedure manuals or participation in creation and maintenance of planning documents such as capacity or availability plans.

3.8   SERVICE OPERATION INPUTS AND OUTPUTS

The main input to service operation is new or changed services put into production from service transition. The main output is value to the business from services that are delivered in accordance with established SLAs.

4 Service operation processes

4.1 EVENT MANAGEMENT

4.1.1 Purpose and objectives

The purpose of event management is to manage events throughout their lifecycle. This lifecycle of activities to detect events, make sense of them and determine the appropriate control action is coordinated by the event management process.

The objectives of the event management process are to:

- Detect all changes of state that have significance for the management of a configuration item (CI) or IT service
- Determine the appropriate control action for events and ensure that these are communicated to the appropriate functions
- Provide the trigger, or entry point, for the execution of many service operation processes and operations management activities
- Provide the means to compare actual operating performance and behaviour against design standards and SLAs
- Provide a basis for service assurance and reporting, and for service improvement.

4.1.2 Scope

Event management can be applied to any aspect of service management that needs to be controlled including:

- Configuration items (CIs)
- Environmental conditions (e.g. fire and smoke detection)

- Software licence monitoring to ensure legal licence use and allocation
- Security (e.g. intrusion detection)
- Normal activity (e.g. tracking use of an application or server performance).

4.1.3 Value to business

Event management's value to the business is generally indirect; however, it is possible to determine the basis for its value as follows:

- Event management provides mechanisms for early detection of incidents before any actual service outage occurs.
- Event management can signal exceptions that allow teams to perform early response, thus improving the performance of processes.
- Event management provides a basis for automated operations, increasing efficiencies and allowing expensive human resources to be used for more innovative work.

4.1.4 Policies, principles and basic concepts

Examples of event management policies are:

- Event notifications should only go to those responsible for the handling of further actions, to avoid needless notifications to those not directly involved.
- Event management and support should be centralized as much as reasonably possible, to avoid conflicts in management of events.
- All application events should utilize a common set of messaging and logging standards wherever possible.

- Event handling actions should be automated wherever possible to prevent incidents caused by human error.
- A standard classification scheme should be in place that references common handling and escalation processes.
- All recognized events should be captured and logged.

Examples of different types of events are:

- **Informational** Events that indicate a change of state such as completion of a scheduled workload or a user logging in.
- **Warning** Events that signify unusual operational conditions such as a disk log file that is reaching its capacity.
- **Exception** Events that signify unacceptable operational conditions such as a server operating above acceptable utilization rates.

Key considerations for designing event management can include:

- Which CIs and services need to be monitored
- When events should be generated
- What needs to be communicated during events
- Who will be responsible for recognizing, communicating, escalating and taking action on events
- Instrumentation to monitor IT infrastructure and services
- Detection and alert mechanisms that populate the tools used to filter, correlate and escalate events
- Rule sets that define how the event messages will be processed, filtered and evaluated.

4.1.5 Process activities, methods and techniques

The event management process includes the steps shown in Figure 4.1.

Figure 4.1 The event management process

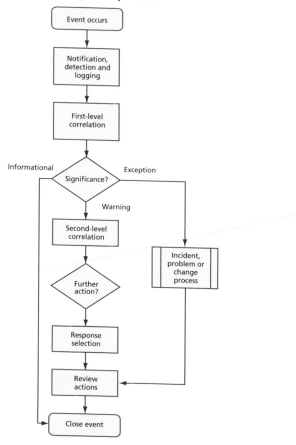

4.1.5.1   Event occurs

Events occur continuously, but not all of them are detected or registered. It is important that everybody involved in designing, developing, managing and supporting IT services and the associated IT infrastructure understands what types of events need to be detected.

4.1.5.2   Event notification

The service design process should define which events need to be generated and specify how this can be done for each type of CI. During service transition, the event generation options would be set and tested.

4.1.5.3   Event detection

Once an event notification has been generated, it will be transmitted directly to a management tool to read and interpret the meaning of the event.

4.1.5.4   Event logged

The event is logged in the event management tool or it can simply be left as an entry in the system log of the device or application that generated the event.

4.1.5.5   First-level event correlation and filtering

The first level of correlation is performed to determine whether the event is informational, a warning, or an exception. Event correlation and filtering determines whether to communicate the event to a management tool or ignore it.

4.1.5.6   Significance of events

The event is categorized by its significance. It is suggested that at least these three broad categories be represented: informational, warning and exception.

4.1.5.7   Second-level event correlation

The second level of correlation compares the event with a set of criteria and business rules in a prescribed order. The idea is that the event may represent some impact on the business and rules can be used to determine the level and type of business impact.

4.1.5.8   Further action required?

If the second-level correlation activity recognizes an event, a response will be required, such as executing a script that performs a specific action.

4.1.5.9   Response selection

A response option is chosen such as rebooting a device, restarting an application, escalating an alert to a person, or initiating the incident, problem or change management process.

4.1.5.10   Review actions

Significant events or exceptions are checked for appropriate handling to ensure that the handover between the event management process and other processes took place as designed. This ensures that incidents, problems or changes originating within operations management do not get lost.

4.1.5.11 Close event

Events that generated an incident, problem or change should be formally closed with a link to the appropriate record from the other process.

4.1.6 Triggers, inputs, outputs and interfaces

Examples of triggers might include:

- Completion of an automated task
- Change of state in a CI.

Examples of inputs may include:

- Alarms, alerts and thresholds for recognizing events
- Event-correlation tables, rules, event codes and automated response solutions that will support event management activities
- Roles and responsibilities for recognizing events and communicating them to those who need to handle them
- Operational procedures for recognizing, logging, escalating and communicating events.

Examples of outputs may include:

- Events that have been communicated and escalated to those responsible for further action
- Event logs describing what events took place to support forensic, diagnosis or further CSI activities
- Events that indicate that an incident has occurred
- Events that indicate the potential breach of an SLA or operational level agreement (OLA) objective
- Events that indicate completion status of deployment, operational or other support activities.

4.1.7   Critical success factors and key performance indicators

Examples of event management critical success factors (CSFs) and key performance indicators (KPIs) include:

- **CSF** Detecting all changes of state that have significance for the management of CIs and IT services
    - **KPI** Number and ratio of events compared with the number of incidents
    - **KPI** Number and percentage of each type of event per platform or application, versus total number of platforms and applications, to identify IT services that lack capability to detect their events
- **CSF** Provide the means to compare actual operating performance and behaviour against design standards and SLAs
    - **KPI** Number and percentage of incidents that were resolved without impact on the business
    - **KPI** Number and percentage of events caused by existing problems or known errors.

4.1.8   Challenges and risks

Challenges for event management include:

- Failure to obtain adequate funding
- Setting the correct level of filtering to avoid being flooded with insignificant events.

Risks to successful event management include:

- Automated monitoring activities can generate additional network traffic that might have negative impacts on capacity levels of the network.

4.2   INCIDENT MANAGEMENT

4.2.1   Purpose and objectives

The purpose of incident management is to restore normal service operation as quickly as possible and minimize the adverse impact on business operations, ensuring that agreed levels of service quality are maintained. 'Normal service operation' is defined as an operational state where services and CIs are performing within their agreed service and operational levels.

The objectives of the incident management process are to:

- Ensure that standardized methods and procedures are used for efficient handling and reporting of incidents
- Increase visibility and communication of incidents to business and IT staff
- Enhance business perception of IT through use of professional approaches in quickly resolving and communicating incidents
- Align incident management activities and priorities with those of the business
- Maintain user satisfaction with the quality of IT services.

4.2.2   Scope

Incident management includes any event which disrupts, or which could disrupt, a service. This includes events which are communicated directly by users, either through the service desk or through an interface from event management to incident management tools.

4.2.3   Value to business

The value of incident management includes:

- The ability to reduce unplanned labour and costs for both the business and IT support staff caused by incidents
- The ability to detect and resolve incidents, which can lower downtime and create higher availability of the service
- The ability to align IT activity to real-time business priorities
- The ability to identify potential improvements to services.

4.2.4   Policies, principles and basic concepts

Examples of incident management policies might include:

- Incidents must be resolved within timeframes acceptable to the business.
- Customer satisfaction must be maintained at all times.
- All incidents should be stored and managed in a single management system.
- All incidents should subscribe to a standard classification schema that is consistent across the business enterprise.
- Incidents should be tracked throughout their lifecycle to support proper handling and reporting on the status of incidents. Examples might include:
  - **Open** An incident has been recognized but not yet assigned to a support resource for resolution.
  - **In progress** The incident is in the process of being investigated and resolved.
  - **Resolved** A resolution has been put in place for the incident, but normal-state service operation has not yet been validated by the business or end user.

– **Closed** The user or business has agreed that the incident has been resolved and that normal-state operations have been restored.

Many incidents are not new – they involve dealing with something that has happened before and may well happen again. For this reason, many organizations will find it helpful to predefine 'standard' incident models and apply them to appropriate incidents when they occur. The incident model should include steps to handle the incident and responsibilities.

A separate procedure, with shorter timescales and greater urgency, must be used for 'major' incidents. A definition of what constitutes a major incident must be agreed and ideally mapped onto the overall incident prioritization scheme – so that these will be dealt with through this separate procedure.

4.2.5 Process activities, methods and techniques

The incident management process includes the steps shown in Figure 4.2.

4.2.5.1 Incident identification

It is unacceptable, from a business perspective, to wait until a user is impacted; therefore all key components should be monitored so that failures or potential failures are detected early.

4.2.5.2 Incident logging

All incidents must be fully logged and date/time stamped, regardless of whether they are raised through a service desk telephone call, automatically detected via an event alert, or come from any other source.

Figure 4.2 Incident management process flow

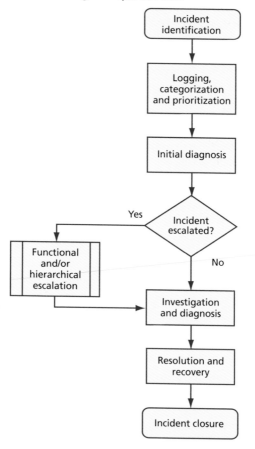

4.2.5.3   Incident categorization

Incidents must be categorized to establish trends for use in problem management, supplier management and other ITSM activities.

4.2.5.4   Incident prioritization

Incidents must be prioritized, taking into account the urgency of the incident (how quickly the business needs a resolution) and the level of business impact it is causing. If circumstances change, or if an incident is not resolved within SLA target times, the priority must be altered to reflect the new situation.

4.2.5.5   Initial diagnosis

If possible, the service desk analyst should resolve an incident while the user is still on the telephone – and close the incident if the resolution and recovery are agreed to be successful.

A procedure can be used for matching incident classification data against problems and known errors. This gives efficient and quick access to proven resolution actions, minimizes the need for escalation to other support staff, and reduces the time it takes to restore service to users. An example of an incident-matching procedure is shown in Figure 4.3.

4.2.5.6   Incident escalation

If the service desk is unable to resolve the incident itself (or when target times for first-point resolution have been exceeded – whichever comes first), the incident must be immediately escalated for further support. Escalation can occur in the following ways:

Figure 4.3 Example of an incident-matching procedure

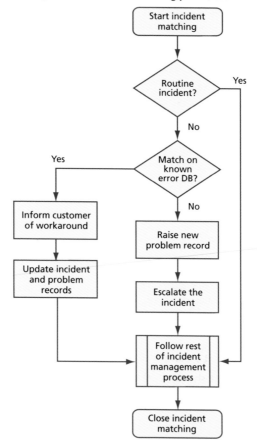

- **Functional escalation** In which the incident is escalated to the next appropriate support group with more time or expertise to resolve the incident.
- **Hierarchical escalation** In which the incident is escalated to senior managers for further action.

Ownership of the incident must remain with the service desk at all times. The service desk remains responsible for tracking progress, keeping users informed and, ultimately, for incident closure.

4.2.5.7   Investigation and diagnosis

Each of the support groups involved with the incident handling will investigate and diagnose what has gone wrong. All such activities are fully documented so that a complete historical record of all activities is maintained.

4.2.5.8   Resolution and recovery

When a potential resolution has been identified, it should be applied. Sufficient testing must be performed to ensure that recovery action is complete and that normal-state service operation has been restored. The incident record is updated so that a full history is maintained. The resolving group should pass the incident back to the service desk for closure action.

4.2.5.9   Incident closure

The service desk should check that the incident is fully resolved and that the users are satisfied and willing to agree the incident can be closed. The incident should then be formally closed.

4.2.6   Triggers, inputs, outputs and interfaces

Examples of incident management triggers can include:

- Users who contact the service desk
- Events raised by event management tools
- Technical staff who notice potential failures and raise an incident
- Suppliers who send notification of a difficulty that needs attention.

Examples of inputs to the incident management process may include:

- Information about known errors and their workarounds
- Communication and feedback about requests for change (RFCs) and releases that have been implemented or planned for implementation
- Communication of events that were triggered from event management
- Operational and service level objectives
- Customer feedback on success of incident resolution activities and overall quality of incident management activities.

Examples of outputs from the incident management process may include:

- Resolved incidents, and actions taken to achieve their resolution
- Updated incident management records with accurate incident detail and history
- Raising of problem records for incidents where an underlying cause has not been identified
- Feedback on incidents related to changes and releases
- Identification of CIs associated with or impacted by incidents

■ Satisfaction feedback from customers who have experienced incidents.

Examples of interfaces with incident management can include:

■ **Service level management** To define measurable responses to service disruptions and provide reports that enable service level management (SLM) to review SLAs objectively and regularly.

■ **Information security management** To support service design activities and gain a full picture of the effectiveness of the security measures as a whole.

■ **Capacity management** To provide a trigger for performance monitoring where there appears to be a performance problem.

■ **Availability management** To determine the availability of IT services and look at where the incident lifecycle can be improved.

■ **Service asset and configuration management** To identify the data needed to identify and progress incidents.

■ **Change management** To log RFCs as resolutions are progressed and resolve incidents that arise from failed changes.

■ **Problem management** To resolve the underlying cause and prevent or reduce the impact of recurrence. Problem management, in return, can provide known errors for faster incident resolution.

■ **Access management** To raise incidents when unauthorized access attempts and security breaches have been detected, and support forensic investigation activities.

4.2.7   Critical success factors and key performance indicators

Examples of incident management CSFs and KPIs can include:

- **CSF** Resolve incidents as quickly as possible, minimizing impacts to the business
    - **KPI** Mean elapsed time to achieve incident resolution or circumvention, broken down by impact code
    - **KPI** Breakdown of incidents at each stage (e.g. logged, work in progress, closed etc.)
    - **KPI** Percentage of incidents closed by the service desk without reference to other levels of support (often referred to as 'first point of contact')
- **CSF** Maintain quality of IT services
    - **KPI** Number and percentage of major incidents for each IT service
- **CSF** Maintain user satisfaction with IT services
    - **KPI** Average user/customer survey score (total and by question category)

4.2.8   Challenges and risks

Challenges for incident management include:

- The ability to detect incidents as early as possible
- Convincing all staff that all incidents must be logged
- Availability of information about problems and known errors
- Integration into the configuration management system (CMS) to determine relationships between CIs, and to refer to the history of CIs when performing first-line support.

Risks to successful incident management include:

■ Being inundated with incidents that cannot be handled within acceptable timescales due to a lack of available or properly trained resources.

4.3   REQUEST FULFILMENT

4.3.1   Purpose and objectives

Request fulfilment is the process responsible for managing the lifecycle of all service requests from users.

The objectives of the request fulfilment process are to:

■ Maintain user and customer satisfaction through efficient and professional handling of all service requests
■ Provide a channel for users to request and receive standard services for which a predefined authorization and qualification process exists
■ Provide information to users and customers about the availability of services and the procedure for obtaining them.

4.3.2   Scope

The process needed to fulfil a request will vary depending upon what is being requested, but it can usually be broken down into a set of activities that have to be performed. For each request, these activities should be documented into a request model and stored in the SKMS.

Note that ultimately it will be up to each organization to decide which processes and functions will handle each service request. For example, the business relationship management process might handle requests for new or changed services.

4.3.3 Value to business

The value of the request fulfilment process includes:

- Providing quick and effective access to standard services that business staff can use to improve their productivity
- Reducing the bureaucracy and costs involved in requesting and receiving access to services
- Reducing costs through centralized negotiation with suppliers.

4.3.4 Policies, principles and basic concepts

Examples of request fulfilment policies might include:

- Activities used to fulfil a request should follow a predefined process flow (a model) that includes the stages needed to fulfil the request, the individuals or support groups involved, timescales and escalation paths.
- The ownership of service requests should reside with a centralized function which monitors, escalates, despatches and often fulfils the user request.
- Service requests that impact CIs should be satisfied by implementing a standard change.
- All requests should be logged, controlled, coordinated, promoted and managed throughout their lifecycle via a single system.
- All requests should be authorized before their fulfilment activities are undertaken.

Examples of basic things that need to be taken into account when considering request fulfilment include:

- **Request models** Define the steps, activities and responsibilities for fulfilling requests.

- **Menu selection** Offer a web-based interface allowing users to select and input details of service requests from a predefined list.
- **Request status tracking** Track requests throughout their lifecycle.
- **Prioritizing requests** Assess the priority of requests.
- **Escalating requests** Establish a mechanism to resolve situations or take further actions that are not part of the standard set of fulfilment activities.
- **Financial approval** The cost of fulfilling the service request must first be established and agreed.
- **Coordination of fulfilment activities** Fulfilment activities should be harmonized across specialist groups and/or suppliers.
- **Closure** The service desk goes through a closure process that checks to see whether the user is satisfied with the outcome.

4.3.5 Process activities, methods and techniques

The request fulfilment process includes the steps shown in Figure 4.4.

4.3.5.1 Receive request

Fulfilment work on service requests should not begin until a formalized request has been received.

4.3.5.2 Request logging and validation

All service requests must be logged and date/time stamped, regardless of whether they are raised through a service desk, RFC, telephone call or email. As further activities to fulfil a request occur, the request record should be updated so that a

Figure 4.4 The request fulfilment process

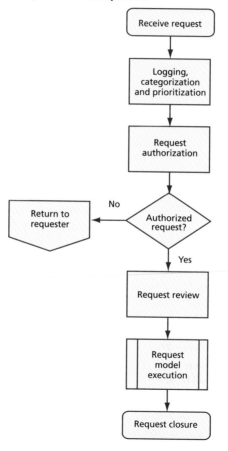

full history is maintained. The source of the request must be validated and checks made to ensure that it is within the scope of the IT services being offered.

4.3.5.3 Request categorization

Part of the initial logging must be to allocate suitable request categorization coding so that the exact type of the request is recorded. This will be important later when looking at request types/frequencies to establish trends in determining how services are being used.

4.3.5.4 Request prioritization

Requests must be prioritized considering both the urgency of the request (how quickly the business needs to have it fulfilled) and the level of impact it is causing.

4.3.5.5 Request authorization

No work should take place to fulfil a request until it has been properly authorized. A service request that cannot be properly authorized should be returned to the requester with the reason for rejection and the request record also updated to indicate the rejection status.

4.3.5.6 Request review

At this stage, the request is reviewed to determine the proper function that will fulfil it. As requests are reviewed, escalated and acted upon, the request records should be updated to reflect the current request status.

4.3.5.7   Request model execution

As functions undertake activities to fulfil a request, a request model should be used that documents a standard process flow, roles and responsibilities for fulfilling it. This ensures that a repeatable and consistent set of actions are always undertaken for each request type to minimize the risk of delays or failures as requests are fulfilled.

4.3.5.8   Request closure

Once service request activities have been completed, the service desk should be notified of the completion status. The service desk should then check that the request has been fulfilled and that users are satisfied and willing to agree that the request can be closed and billed for if appropriate.

4.3.5.9   Rules for reopening requests

It is wise to have predefined rules covering if and when a closed service request can be reopened. Clear rules should be agreed and documented and guidance given to all service desk staff so that uniformity is applied.

4.3.6   Triggers, inputs, outputs and interfaces

Most requests will be triggered through either a user calling the service desk or a user completing some form of self-help web-based input screen to make their request.

Examples of inputs to the request fulfilment process can include:

- Work requests
- Authorization forms
- Service requests

- RFCs
- Requests from various sources such as phone calls, web interfaces or email.

Examples of outputs from the request fulfilment process may include:

- Request fulfilment status reports
- Fulfilled service requests
- Updated request records
- Closed service requests
- Cancelled service requests.

Examples of interfaces with request fulfilment are listed below:

- **Financial management for IT services** May be needed if costs for fulfilling requests have to be reported and recovered.
- **Service catalogue management** Will need to ensure that available requests are communicated to users and linked with the services in the catalogue that they support.
- **Service asset and configuration management** Will have to update the CMS to reflect changes that may have been made as part of fulfilment activities.
- **Access management** May be involved with request fulfilment activities to ensure that those making requests are authorized to do so in accordance with the information security policy.

4.3.7 Critical success factors and key performance indicators

Examples of request fulfilment CSFs and KPIs can include:

- **CSF** Requests must be fulfilled in an efficient and timely manner that is aligned to agreed service level targets for each type of request

- – **KPI** The mean elapsed time for handling each type of service request
- – **KPI** The number and percentage of service requests completed within agreed target times
- **CSF** Only authorized requests should be fulfilled
  - – **KPI** Percentage of service requests fulfilled that were appropriately authorized
- **CSF** User satisfaction must be maintained
  - – **KPI** Level of user satisfaction with the handling of service requests (as measured in some form of satisfaction survey).

4.3.8 Challenges and risks

Challenges for request fulfilment include:

- Clearly defining and documenting the type of requests that will be handled within the request fulfilment process so that all parties are absolutely clear on the scope
- Establishing self-help front-end capabilities that allow users to interface successfully with the request fulfilment process
- Agreeing the costs for fulfilling requests
- Agreeing which services will be standardized and who is authorized to request them.

Risks to successful request fulfilment include:

- Badly designed or operated back-end fulfilment processes that are incapable of dealing with the volume or nature of the requests being made.

4.4   PROBLEM MANAGEMENT

4.4.1   Purpose and objectives

ITIL defines a 'problem' as the underlying cause of one or more incidents. The purpose of problem management is to manage the lifecycle of all problems from first identification through further investigation, documentation and eventual removal. Problem management seeks to get to the root cause of incidents, document and communicate known errors, and initiate actions to improve or correct the situation.

The objectives of the problem management process are to:

■ Prevent problems and resulting incidents from happening
■ Eliminate recurring incidents
■ Minimize the impact of incidents that cannot be prevented.

4.4.2   Scope

Problem management includes the activities required to diagnose the root cause of incidents and to determine the resolution to those problems. It is also responsible for ensuring that the resolution is implemented through the appropriate control procedures; especially change management and release and deployment management.

Problem management will also maintain information about problems and the appropriate workarounds and resolutions, so that the organization is able to reduce the number and impact of incidents over time.

The problem management process has both reactive and proactive aspects:

- **Reactive problem management** Concerned with solving problems in response to one or more incidents
- **Proactive problem management** Concerned with identifying and solving problems and known errors before further related incidents can occur again.

Proactive problem management supports those activities through trending analysis and the targeting of preventive action. Identified problems from these activities will provide input to the CSI register to record and manage improvement opportunities.

4.4.3 Value to business

The value of problem management includes:

- Higher availability of IT services by reducing the number and duration of incidents
- Higher productivity of IT staff by reducing unplanned labour caused by incidents, and resolving incidents more quickly through recorded known errors and workarounds
- Reduced expenditure on workarounds or fixes that do not work.

4.4.4 Policies, principles and basic concepts

Examples of problem management policies might include:

- Problems should be tracked separately from incidents to provide clear separation between many problem management activities, which are proactive, and incident management activities, which are mostly reactive.
- All problems should be stored and managed in a single management system that tracks problems separately from incidents.

■ All problems should subscribe to a standard classification schema that is consistent across the business enterprise with a well-defined and communicated set of problem classification categories in place.

4.4.4.1 Principles and basic concepts

There are some important concepts of problem management that must be taken into account from the outset. These include:

■ **Reactive and proactive problem management activities** Find the underlying causes of the incidents they are associated with and prevent future recurrences of those incidents.
■ **Problem models** Ensure quicker diagnosis through the creation of predefined investigative and resolution activities.

Examples of frequently used techniques to assist with management of problems and finding their root causes can include:

■ **Chronological analysis** Provides a timeline of events to show which events may have been triggered by others.
■ **Pain value analysis** Determines exactly what level of pain has been caused to the business by incidents, and prioritizes resolution actions.
■ **Kepner and Tregoe approach** Methods (developed by Charles Kepner and Benjamin Tregoe) used to define problems, establish possible causes, test and verify the true cause.
■ **Brainstorming** Sessions in which people suggest ideas on potential causes and actions to resolve problems.
■ **5-Whys approach** A method that gets to the root cause by starting out with a description of the event that took place and then repeatedly asking why this occurred.

- **Fault isolation** An approach that re-executes transactions or events in a careful stepwise fashion, one CI at a time, until the CI at fault is identified.
- **Affinity mapping** Organizes data (ideas, opinions, issues) under headings that are examined for potential root causes which may underlie all of the problems.
- **Hypothesis testing** Lists possible root causes based on educated guesses, and then determines whether each hypothesis is true or false.
- **Technical observation post** Monitors events, real-time as they occur, with the specific aim of catching and identifying problem causes.
- **Ishikawa diagrams** (Developed by Kaoru Ishikawa, a leader in Japanese quality control) show causes and effects to explain a complex problem.

4.4.5 Process activities, methods and techniques

The problem management process includes the steps shown in Figure 4.5.

4.4.5.1 Problem detection

Problems are triggered through reactive and proactive problem management.

Reactive problem management triggers:

- Suspicion or detection of a cause of one or more incidents by the service desk.
- A technical support group reveals that an underlying problem exists.
- Events and alerts that automatically raise an incident which may require the creation of a problem record.

Figure 4.5 The problem management process

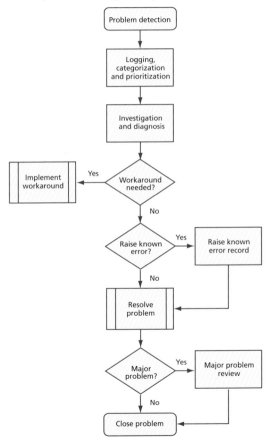

■ A notification from a supplier or contractor that a problem exists.

Proactive problem management triggers:

■ Analysis of incidents that result in the need to raise a problem record.
■ Trending of historical incident records to identify underlying causes that, if removed, can prevent recurrence.
■ Activities to improve the quality of a service that result in the need to raise a problem record.

4.4.5.2 Problem logging

Regardless of the detection method, all the relevant details of the problem must be recorded so that a full historic record exists.

4.4.5.3 Problem categorization

Problems should be categorized in the same way as incidents (and it is advisable to use the same coding system) so that problems can be easily traced and matched so that meaningful management information can be obtained.

4.4.5.4 Problem prioritization

Problems should be prioritized the same way using the same reasons as for incidents. A coding system which combines frequency and impact of related incidents with urgency should also be used to prioritize problems.

4.4.5.5 Problem investigation and diagnosis

An investigation is conducted to diagnose the root cause of the problem. Appropriate levels of resources and expertise should be applied to finding a resolution commensurate with the priority code allocated and the service target in place for that priority level.

4.4.5.6   Workarounds

In some cases it may be possible to find a temporary workaround for the incidents caused by the problem. When a workaround is found, the problem record remains open and details of the workaround are documented within the problem record.

4.4.5.7   Raising a known error record

A known error is defined as a problem with a documented root cause and workaround. A known error record must be raised and placed in the known error database (KEDB) so that if further incidents or problems arise, the service can be restored more quickly.

4.4.5.8   Problem resolution

Once a root cause has been found and a resolution developed to remove it, that solution should be applied to resolve the problem. An RFC should be raised and authorized before the resolution can be applied. The resolution should be implemented only when the change has been authorized and scheduled for release.

4.4.5.9   Problem closure

When a final resolution has been applied, the problem record should be formally closed – as should any related incident records that are still open. The status of any related known error record should be updated to show that the resolution has been put in place.

4.4.5.10 Major problem review

After every major problem (as determined by the organization's priority system), a review should be conducted to learn any lessons for the future. Specifically, the review should examine:

- Things that were done correctly
- Things that were done wrong
- What could be done better in the future
- How to prevent recurrence
- Any third-party responsibility and whether follow-up actions are needed.

4.4.6   Triggers, inputs, outputs and interfaces

With reactive problem management, the vast majority of problem records will be triggered in reaction to one or more incidents. Suppliers may trigger problems through the notification of known deficiencies in their products or services.

With proactive problem management, problem records may be triggered by identification of patterns and trends in incidents when reviewing historical incident records, operation or event logs.

Examples of inputs to the problem management process may include:

- Incident records that have triggered problem management activities
- Incident reports used to support proactive problem trending

■ Communication about RFCs and releases that have been
   implemented or planned for implementation

■ Agreed criteria for prioritizing and escalating problems.

Examples of outputs from the problem management process
may include:

■ Resolved problems and actions taken to achieve their
   resolution

■ Updated problem management records

■ RFCs to remove infrastructure errors

■ Known error records

■ Problem management reports.

Examples of key interfaces are:

■ **IT Financial management** Provides the cost of resolving and
   preventing problems.

■ **Availability management** Uses problem management
   information to identify issues and failure points.

■ **Service level management** Uses problem management
   information to identify improvements in service levels.

■ **Service asset and configuration management** Identifies
   faulty CIs and determines the impact of problems and
   resolutions.

■ **The seven-step improvement process** Uses problem
   management information as a basis for identifying
   opportunities for service improvement and adding them to
   the CSI register.

4.4.7   Critical success factors and key performance indicators

Examples of problem management CSFs and KPIs can include:

- **CSF** Minimize the impact to the business of incidents that cannot be prevented
  - **KPI** The number of known errors added to the KEDB
  - **KPI** Average incident resolution time for those incidents linked to problem records
- **CSF** Maintain quality of IT services through elimination of recurring incidents
  - **KPI** Total numbers of problems (as a control measure)
  - **KPI** Number of repeat incidents for each IT service
- **CSF** Provide overall quality and professionalism of problem-handling activities to maintain business confidence in IT capabilities
  - **KPI** The backlog of outstanding problems and the trend (static, reducing or increasing?)
  - **KPI** Number and percentage of problems that exceeded their target resolution times.

4.4.8   Challenges and risks

Challenges for problem management include:

- Establishment of an effective incident management process and tools to ensure that formal incident and problem interfaces and common working practices are in place
- Ensuring that problem resolution staff have the skills and capabilities to identify the true root cause of incidents
- Making sure that business impact is well understood by all staff working on problem resolution.

Risks to successful problem management include:

- Being inundated with problems that cannot be handled within acceptable timescales due to a lack of available or properly trained resources.

4.5   ACCESS MANAGEMENT

4.5.1   Purpose and objectives

The purpose of access management is to provide users with the right to be able to use a service or group of services. It is therefore the execution of policies and actions defined in information security management.

The objectives of the access management process are to:

- Manage access to services based on policies and actions defined in information security management
- Efficiently respond to requests for granting access to services, changing access rights or restricting access, ensuring that the rights are being properly granted
- Oversee access to services and ensure that rights being provided are not improperly used.

4.5.2   Scope

Access management is the execution of the policies in information security management, in that it enables the organization to manage the confidentiality, availability and integrity of the organization's data and intellectual property.

Access management is a process that is executed by all technical and application management functions, and there is likely to be a single control point of coordination, usually in IT operations management or on the service desk.

4.5.3   Value to business

The value of access management includes:

- Ensuring that controlled access to services allows the organization to maintain effective confidentiality of its information
- Ensuring that employees have the right level of access to execute their jobs effectively
- Providing capabilities to audit use of services and to trace the abuse of services
- Providing capabilities to revoke access rights when needed on a timely basis – an important security consideration
- Providing and demonstrating compliance with regulatory requirements (e.g. SOX, HIPAA and COBIT).

4.5.4 Policies, principles and basic concepts

Examples of access management policies might include:

- Access management activities should be guided and directed by the policies and controls as defined in the information security policy
- Access management should log and track accesses to use of services and ensure that rights being provided are appropriately used
- Access management should maintain access to services in alignment with changes in personnel events such as transfers and terminations
- Access management should maintain an accurate history of who has accessed, or tried to access, services
- Procedures for handling, escalating and communicating security events should be clearly defined and documented in accordance with the information security policy.

Access management comprises the following basic concepts:

- **Access** Refers to the level and extent of a service's functionality or data that a user is entitled to use.
- **Identity** Refers to the information about users that distinguishes them as individuals and verifies their status within the organization.
- **Rights (also called privileges)** Refer to the actual settings whereby a user is granted access to a service or group of services.
- **Directory services** Refer to specific types of tools that are used to manage access and rights.

4.5.5   Process activities, methods and techniques

The access management process includes the steps shown in Figure 4.6.

4.5.5.1   Request access

Access (or restriction) can be requested via:

- A service request
- An RFC
- By executing a pre-authorized script or option.

4.5.5.2   Verification

Access management needs to verify requests for access from two perspectives:

- Whether the user requesting access is who they say they are
- Whether the user has a legitimate requirement for that service.

Figure 4.6 Access management process

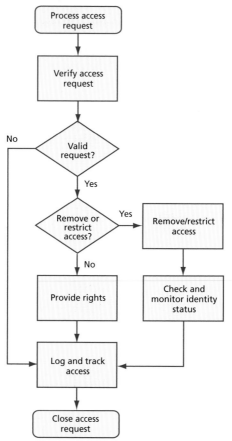

4.5.5.3   Provide rights

Access management enforces decisions to restrict or provide access, rather than making the decision. As soon as a user has been verified, access management will provide that user with rights to use the requested service.

4.5.5.4   Check and monitor identity status

Procedures and activities should be in place to monitor changes to user roles in the organization and their need to access services. Examples can include job changes, promotions, transfers, disciplinary actions or dismissals.

4.5.5.5   Log and track access

Access management is responsible for ensuring that the rights they have provided are being properly used. In this respect, access monitoring and control must be included in the monitoring activities of all technical and application management functions and all service operation processes.

Access management may also be required to provide a record of access for specific services during forensic investigations. If a user is suspected of breaches of policy, inappropriate use of resources or fraudulent use of data, access management may be required to provide evidence of dates, times and even content of that user's access to specific services.

4.5.5.6   Remove or restrict rights

Access rights should be removed from users who have left the business organization. These rights may be restricted in circumstances where users have changed organization roles or are temporarily on leave.

4.5.6 Triggers, inputs, outputs and interfaces

Access management is triggered by a request for a user or users to access a service or group of services. This could originate from:

- An RFC
- A service request
- A request from human resources.

Examples of inputs to access management may include:

- Information security policies
- Operational and service level requirements for granting access to services, performing access management administrative activities and responding to access management-related events
- Authorized requests to grant or terminate access rights.

Examples of outputs from access management may include:

- Provision, removal or changes of access to IT services in accordance with information security policies
- Access management records and history of access granted to services
- Access management records and history where access has been denied and the reasons for the denial
- Communications and security-related incident information concerning inappropriate access or abuse of services.

Examples of interfaces with other processes are:

- **Information security management** Provides security and data protection policies and tools needed to execute access management.

- **Service catalogue management** Provides methods and means by which users can access different IT services, service descriptions and views for which they are authorized.
- **IT service continuity management** Interfaces may be needed to manage access to services in the event of a major business disruption or in conditions where services have been temporarily sourced from alternative locations.
- **Change management** Controls the actual requests for access.
- **Request fulfilment** Provides methods and means by which users can request access to the standard services that are available to them.

4.5.7   Critical success factors and key performance indicators

Examples of access management CSFs and KPIs can include:

- **CSF** Ensuring that the confidentiality, integrity and availability of services are protected in accordance with the information security policy
  - **KPI** Percentage of incidents that involved inappropriate security access or attempts at access to services
  - **KPI** Number of audit findings that discovered incorrect access settings for users who have changed roles or left the company
- **CSF** Provide appropriate access to services on a timely basis to meet business needs
  - **KPI** Percentage of requests for access (service request, RFC etc.) that were provided within established SLAs and OLAs
- **CSF** Provide communications about improper access or abuse of services on a timely basis
  - **KPI** Average duration of access-related incidents (from time of discovery to escalation).

4.5.8 Challenges and risks

Challenges for access management include:

- Verifying the identity of a user (that the person is who they say they are)
- Verifying that a user qualifies for access to a specific service
- Determining the status of users at any time (e.g. to determine whether they are still employees of the organization when they log on to a system)
- Managing changes to a user's access requirements
- Restricting access rights to authorized users.

Risks to successful access management include:

- Controlling access from 'back-door' sources such as application interfaces and changes to firewall rules for special needs
- Managing and controlling access to services by external third-party suppliers.

5 Organizing for service operation

There is no single best way to organize, and best practices described in ITIL need to be tailored to suit each situation, taking into account resource constraints and the size, nature and needs of the business and customers. The starting point for organizational design is service strategy.

Section 2.2.3 of this publication provides an overview of functions and roles.

5.1 FUNCTIONS

For service operation to be successful, an organization will need to define the roles and responsibilities required to undertake the processes and activities identified in this key element guide. These roles should be assigned to individuals, and an appropriate organization structure of teams, groups or functions established and managed.

5.1.1 Service desk function

The primary aim of the service desk is to provide a single point of contact between the services being provided and the users. A typical service desk manages incidents and service requests, and also handles communication with the users.

Specific responsibilities include:

- Logging all relevant incident/service request details, allocating categorization and prioritization codes
- Providing first-line investigation and diagnosis
- Resolving incidents/service requests when first contacted whenever possible

- Escalating incidents/service requests that they cannot resolve within agreed timescales
- Closing all resolved incidents, requests and other calls
- Conducting customer/user satisfaction call-backs/surveys as agreed
- Communication with users – keeping them informed of incident progress, notifying them of impending changes or agreed outages etc.

There are many ways of structuring service desks. Examples include:

- **Local service desk** A desk that is co-located within or physically close to the user community it serves.
- **Centralized service desk** It is possible to reduce the number of service desks by merging them into a single location (or into a smaller number of locations) by drawing the staff into one or more centralized service desk structures.
- **Virtual service desk** It is possible to give the impression of a single centralized service desk through the use of technology, when in fact the personnel may be spread or located in any number or type of geographical or structural locations.
- **Follow the sun** Some global organizations may wish to combine two or more of their geographically dispersed service desks to provide a 24-hour follow-the-sun service (e.g. a service desk in the Asia-Pacific region may handle calls during standard office hours then transfer responsibility for any open incidents to a European-based desk after that time, which in turn passes them over to a USA-based desk, which finally hands back responsibility to the Asia-Pacific desk to complete the cycle).

■ **Specialized service desk groups** These consist of specialist groups within the overall service desk structure; incidents relating to a particular IT service can be routed directly to them.

Examples of service desk metrics can include:

■ Percentage of calls resolved during the first contact with the service desk
■ Percentage of calls resolved by the service desk staff without having to escalate to other support groups
■ Average time to resolve an incident
■ Average cost of handling an incident
■ Number of calls broken down by time of day and day of week
■ Customer satisfaction with service desk performance.

5.1.2   Technical management function

Technical management provides technical skills and resources needed to support the ongoing delivery of IT services and management of the IT infrastructure. The objectives of technical management are to plan, implement and maintain a stable technical infrastructure to support the organization's business processes through:

■ Well-designed and highly resilient, cost-effective technical topology
■ Use of adequate technical skills to maintain the technical infrastructure in optimum condition
■ Application of technical skills to speedily diagnose and resolve technical failures that do occur.

Examples of technical management activities can include:

- Identifying the knowledge and expertise required to manage and operate the IT infrastructure and to deliver IT services
- Initiating training programmes to develop and refine appropriate technical resource skills
- Procuring skills for specific activities where the required skills are not available internally
- Defining the standards to be used for architectures and participating service strategy and design stages
- Researching and developing solutions that expand the service portfolio, automate IT operations, reduce costs or increase levels of IT service
- Assessing risk, and implementing countermeasures
- Participating in resolution of incidents and problems
- Supporting the change management process where reliance on technical knowledge and expertise may be needed to evaluate changes.

The primary criterion of technical management organizational structure is that of specialization or division of labour. The principle is that people are grouped according to their technical skill sets, and that these skill sets are determined by the technology that needs to be managed.

Examples of technical management metrics can include:

- Response time to events and event completion rates
- Incident resolution times for second- and third-line support
- Problem resolution statistics
- Number of escalations and reason for those escalations
- Tracking against service improvement plans (SIPs).

5.1.3   IT operations function

This function executes the set of activities involved in the day-to-day running of the IT infrastructure for the purpose of delivering IT services at agreed levels to meet stated business objectives. The function has two sub-functions:

■ **IT operations control** Oversees the execution and monitoring of operational activities and events in the IT infrastructure. It performs the following specific tasks:
  - Managing the operations bridge to exercise event management, monitoring and control activities
  - Job scheduling, or the management of routine batch jobs or scripts
  - Backup and restore on behalf of all technical/application management teams and departments and users
  - Print and output management for the collation and distribution of all centralized printing or electronic output
  - Server, mainframe and network management and support
  - Performance of maintenance activities for technical/ application management teams or departments.
■ **Facilities management** Provides management of the physical IT environment, typically a data centre, computer rooms or recovery sites together with all the power and cooling equipment.

The objectives of IT operations management include:

■ Achieving stability of the organization's day-to-day processes and activities
■ Achieving improved service at reduced costs, while maintaining stability

■ Applying swift application of operational skills to diagnose and resolve any IT operations failures that occur.

Examples of IT operations management key metrics can include:

■ Percentage of scheduled jobs completed successfully on time
■ Number of exceptions to scheduled activities and jobs
■ Equipment installation statistics, including number of items installed by type, successful installations etc.
■ Maintenance performed per schedule
■ Thresholds and monitoring results for environmental factors such as heating and air conditioning.

5.1.4   Application management function

Application management is responsible for managing applications throughout their lifecycle. It covers lifecycle activities including requirements, design, build, deploy, operate and optimize. Application management differs from application development in that it provides ongoing management of applications, while application development is mainly concerned with one-time activities for requirements, design and build of applications.

The objectives of application management are to:

■ Support the organization's business processes by helping to identify functional and manageability requirements for application software
■ Assist application development in the design and deployment of applications
■ Provide ongoing support and improvement of applications
■ Maintain technical skills to manage, maintain and support applications

■ Quickly diagnose and resolve any application failures that do occur.

The application management lifecycle is illustrated in Figure 5.1.

Figure 5.1 Application management lifecycle

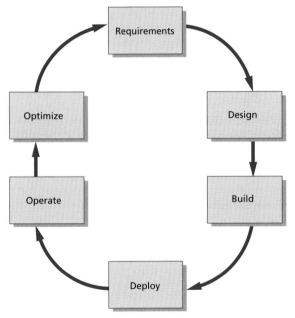

5.1.4.1   Requirements

Requirements for a new application are gathered, based on the business needs of the organization.

5.1.4.2   Design

Requirements are translated into specifications. Design includes the design of the application itself and the environment or operational model that the application has to run on. Design for purchased software will include the design of any customization that is required.

5.1.4.3   Build

The application and the operational model are made ready for deployment. Application components are coded or acquired, integrated and tested. For purchased software, this involves the purchase of the application, any required middleware and the related hardware and networking equipment.

5.1.4.4   Deploy

The application and the operational model (specification of the operational environment in which the application will eventually run when it goes live) are deployed. The operational model is incorporated into the existing IT environment and the application is installed on top of the operational model.

5.1.4.5   Operate

The IT services organization monitors, manages, maintains and operates the application as part of delivering a service required by the business.

Organizing for service operation

5.1.4.6 Optimize

Application-related service level performance measurements are measured, analysed and acted upon. The two main strategies in this stage are to maintain and/or improve the service levels and to lower cost. This could lead to iteration in the lifecycle or to justified retirement of an application.

Examples of application management activities can include:

- Recruiting or contracting resources with skills to perform required application management activities such as bug tracking, design, build and patch management
- Designing and delivering end-user training
- Designing and performing tests for the functionality, performance and manageability of IT services
- Managing contracts with suppliers of specific applications
- Supporting change management with application knowledge and expertise to evaluate changes
- Participating in release and deployment management activities
- Defining the operational activities related to applications that will be performed as part of IT operations management
- Providing third-level support for incidents related to the applications.

Examples of measurements for the application management function can include:

- Incident resolution times for second- and third-line support
- Number of releases deployed, total and successful, including ensuring adherence to the release policies of the organization
- Tracking against SIPs
- Maintenance performed per schedule

- Time spent on projects
- Customer and user satisfaction with the output of the project
- Percentage of incidents caused by skills issues.

5.2 ROLES

A number of roles need to be performed in support of service operation. The core ITIL publications provide guidelines and examples of role descriptions. In many cases roles will need to be combined or separated depending on the organizational context and size.

A RACI model can be used to define the roles and responsibilities in relation to processes and activities.

RACI is an acronym for:

- **Responsible** The person or people responsible for correct execution – for getting the job done.
- **Accountable** The person who has ownership of quality and the end result.
- **Consulted** The people who are consulted and whose opinions are sought. They have involvement through input of knowledge and information.
- **Informed** The people who are kept up to date on progress. They receive information about process execution and quality.

Only one person should be accountable for any process or individual activity, although several people may be responsible for executing parts of the activity.

Roles fall into two main categories – generic roles such as process manager and process owner, and specific roles that are involved within a particular lifecycle stage or process, such as a change administrator or knowledge management process owner.

5.2.1   Generic service owner role

The service owner is accountable for the delivery of a specific IT service and is responsible for the initiation, transition, maintenance and support of that service.

The service owner's responsibilities include:

- Working with business relationship management to ensure that the service provider can meet customer requirements
- Participating in negotiating service level agreements (SLAs) and operational level agreements (OLAs) relating to the service
- Ensuring that ongoing service delivery and support meet agreed customer requirements
- Ensuring consistent and appropriate communication with customer(s) for service-related enquiries and issues
- Representing the service across the organization, including at change advisory board (CAB) meetings
- Serving as the point of escalation (notification) for major incidents relating to the service
- Participating in internal and external service review meetings.

The service owner is responsible for continual improvement and the management of change affecting the service under their care.

5.2.2 Generic process owner role

The process owner role is accountable for ensuring that a process is fit for purpose, is performed according to agreed standards and meets the aims of the process definition. This role is often assigned to the same person who carries out the process manager role, but the two roles may be separate in larger organizations.

The process owner's accountabilities include:

■ Sponsoring, designing and change managing the process and its metrics

■ Defining appropriate policies and standards for the process, with periodic auditing to ensure compliance

■ Providing process resources to support activities required throughout the service lifecycle

■ Ensuring that process technicians understand their role and have the required knowledge to deliver the process

■ Addressing issues with running the process

■ Identifying enhancement and improvement opportunities and making improvements to the process.

5.2.3 Generic process manager role

The process manager role is accountable for operational management of a process. There may be several process managers for one process, for example covering different locations.

The process manager's accountabilities include:

■ Working with the process owner to plan and coordinate all process activities

- Ensuring that all activities are carried out as required throughout the service lifecycle
- Appointing people to the required roles and managing assigned resources
- Monitoring and reporting on process performance
- Identifying opportunities for and making improvements to the process.

5.2.4 Generic process practitioner role

The process practitioner's responsibilities include:

- Carrying out one or more activities of a process
- Understanding how their role contributes to the overall delivery of service and creation of value for the business
- Ensuring that inputs, outputs and interfaces for their activities are correct
- Creating or updating records to show that activities have been carried out correctly.

5.2.5 Event management roles

5.2.5.1 Event management process owner

The event management process owner responsibilities include:

- Carrying out the generic process owner role for the event management process
- Planning and managing support for event management tools and processes
- Working with other process owners to ensure that there is an integrated approach to the design and implementation of event management and the other service operation processes.

5.2.5.2 Event management process manager

This role provides support for event management tools and processes, and coordinates interfaces between event management and other service management processes.

The event management process manager responsibilities include:

- Liaising with all service support functions to ensure that events are properly communicated
- Establishing appropriate levels of alarms, alerts and thresholds that trigger events
- Handling requests to add, modify or delete events as needed.

5.2.6 Incident management roles

5.2.6.1 Incident management process owner

The incident management process owner responsibilities include:

- Carrying out the generic process owner role for the incident management process
- Designing incident models and workflows
- Working with other process owners to ensure that there is an integrated approach to the design and implementation of incident management and the other service operation processes.

5.2.6.2 Incident management process manager

This role plans and manages support for incident management tools and processes.

The incident management process manager responsibilities include:

- Producing incident management information
- Managing the work of incident support staff
- Managing major incidents
- Developing and maintaining the incident management process and procedures.

5.2.6.3   First-line analyst

This role provides first-line support for incidents when they occur, using the incident management process.

The first-line analyst responsibilities include:

- Recording incidents, routing incidents to support specialist groups when needed
- Analysing incidents for correct prioritization
- Classifying and providing initial support, ownership, monitoring, tracking and communication of incidents.

5.2.6.4   Second-line analyst

Many organizations choose to have a second-line support group, made up of staff with greater technical skills than the service desk – and with additional time to devote to incident diagnosis and resolution without interference from telephone interruptions.

The second-line analyst responsibilities are similar to the first-line analyst responsibilities.

5.2.6.5 Third-line analyst

Third-line support consists of a number of internal technical groups and/or third-party suppliers/maintainers. Depending upon where an organization decides to source its support services, any of these groups could be internal or external groups.

The third-line analyst responsibilities are similar to the first-line analyst responsibilities.

5.2.7 Request fulfilment roles

5.2.7.1 Request fulfilment process owner

The request fulfilment process owner responsibilities include:

- Carrying out the generic process owner role for the request fulfilment process
- Designing request fulfilment models and workflows
- Working with other process owners to ensure that there is an integrated approach to the design and implementation of request fulfilment and the other service operation processes.

5.2.7.2 Request fulfilment process manager

This role plans and manages support for request fulfilment tools and processes.

The request fulfilment process manager responsibilities include:

- Handling staff, customer and management concerns, requests, issues and enquiries
- Ensuring that request fulfilment activities operate in line with service level targets

- Assisting with activities to appropriately identify staffing resource levels required to handle demand for request fulfilment activities and services
- Representing request fulfilment activities at CAB meetings
- Reviewing the initial prioritization and authorization of service requests to determine accuracy and consistency.

5.2.7.3   Request fulfilment analyst

This role coordinates fulfilment activities for service requests to maintain high levels of satisfaction with IT services.

The request fulfilment analyst responsibilities include:

- Overseeing, managing and coordinating all activities to respond to a service request
- Serving as a single point of contact until requests are fulfilled
- Providing a single point of contact and end-to-end responsibility to ensure that submitted service requests have been processed
- Communicating service requests to other IT resources that will be involved in fulfilling them
- Ensuring that service requests are appropriately logged.

5.2.8   Problem management roles

5.2.8.1   Problem management process owner

The problem management process owner responsibilities include:

- Carrying out the generic process owner role for the problem management process
- Designing problem models and workflows

■ Working with other process owners to ensure that there is an integrated approach to the design and implementation of problem management and the other service operation processes.

5.2.8.2   Problem management process manager

This role plans and manages support for problem management tools and processes.

The problem management process manager responsibilities include:

■ Liaising with all problem resolution groups to ensure swift resolution of problems within SLA targets
■ Formally closing all problem records
■ Arranging, running, documenting and all follow-up activities relating to major problem reviews.

5.2.8.3   Problem analyst

This role reviews incident data to analyse and resolve assigned problems.

The problem analyst responsibilities include:

■ Analysing problems for correct prioritization and classification
■ Investigating assigned problems through to resolution or root cause
■ Raising RFCs to resolve problems
■ Assisting with the handling of major incidents and identifying their root causes.

5.2.9   Access management roles

5.2.9.1   Access management process owner

The access management process owner responsibilities include:

- Carrying out the generic process owner role for the access management process
- Planning and managing support for access management tools and processes
- Designing access request workflows
- Working with other process owners to ensure that there is an integrated approach to the design and implementation of access management and the other service operation processes.

5.2.9.2   Access management process manager

This role provides planning and management support for access management tools and processes.

The access management process manager responsibilities include:

- Coordinating activities to maintain and manage access to IT services
- Coordinating interfaces between access management and other service management processes.

6 Implementing service operation

6.1 MANAGING CHANGE IN SERVICE OPERATION

Service operation staff must ensure that any changes are absorbed without adverse impact upon the stability of the IT services being offered.

Service operation staff must be involved in the assessment of all changes to ensure that operational impact is fully taken into account.

6.2 SERVICE OPERATION AND PROJECT MANAGEMENT

Because service operation is often focused on executing defined procedures in a standard way, formal project management can be used to improve, control and manage costs and resources. Key benefits of using project management can include greater consistency and improved quality, higher confidence and credibility for operations staff, and greater ease of obtaining funding for projects that have traditionally been difficult to justify on grounds of cost.

6.3 ASSESSING AND MANAGING RISK IN SERVICE OPERATION

There will be occasions where it is imperative that risk assessment to service operation is quickly undertaken and acted upon. Key threats to stable operation can come from:

■ Potential changes or known errors

- Failures, or potential failures – either reported by event management, incident/problem management, or warnings raised by manufacturers, suppliers or contractors
- New projects, services or applications being delivered into the live environment
- Environmental risk (encompassing risks to the physical environment and locale as well as political, commercial or industrial relations-related risks)
- Suppliers, where new suppliers are involved or where key service components are under the control of third parties
- Security risks arising from security-related incidents or events.

6.4   OPERATIONAL STAFF IN SERVICE DESIGN AND TRANSITION

Service operation staff must be involved during the early stages of service design and service transition to ensure that when new services reach the live environment they are fit for purpose from a service operation perspective, and are 'supportable' in the future.

6.5   PLANNING AND IMPLEMENTING SERVICE MANAGEMENT TECHNOLOGIES

There are a number of factors that organizations need to plan for in deployment and implementation of ITSM support tools. These include:

- Licences for hardware and software
- Planning and execution for discovery and event-monitoring tools that require client/agent software that must be deployed to all target locations before they can be used

- Ensuring that the capacity of the network can handle the transmission of management information, the transmission of log files and the distribution of clients, and also possibly software and configuration files
- Ensuring that tools are deployed at the appropriate time in relation to the organization's level of ITSM sophistication and knowledge
- Whether to go for a 'Big Bang' introduction or some sort of phased approach.

7 Challenges, risks and critical success factors

7.1 CHALLENGES

There are a number of challenges faced within service operation that include:

- Lack of engagement with development and project staff in thinking of service operation issues at the outset of new developments or projects
- Justifying funding, as money spent in service operation is often regarded as 'infrastructure costs' with nothing new to show for the investment
- Service design may tend to focus on individual services, whereas service operation tends to focus on delivering and supporting all services at the same time
- Operational staff may not be available to participate in service design project activities, which in turn results in IT services that are difficult to operate.

7.2 RISKS

The risks to achieving successful service operation can include:

- Inadequate funding and resources
- Loss of momentum
- Loss of key personnel
- Resistance to change
- Lack of management support
- Faulty design
- Distrust in service management

- Differing customer expectations.

7.3 CRITICAL SUCCESS FACTORS

Critical success factors for service operation can include:

- Management support for ITSM activities and processes
- Business support for service operation activities
- Champions who lead others and communicate their enthusiasm and commitment for ITSM
- Retention of staff with appropriate service operation skills
- Training that instils support staff with a 'service management culture'
- Tools to effect efficient service operation processes and activities
- Measurement and reporting to quickly review progress and pinpoint any areas requiring attention.

8   Key messages and lessons

Key messages and guidance when looking to implement service operation are as follows:

- Success depends on achieving the correct balance between conflicting priorities of internal and external views; stability and responsiveness; quality and cost; and reactive and proactive behaviour.
- Service operation staff need to be involved and engaged in all phases of the service lifecycle to ensure successful design, transition and improvement of services, providing suitable metrics and operational features to meet business needs.
- Understanding the difference between events, incidents, service requests, access requests and problems is essential so that each of these can be handled correctly. It is also important that these processes work together using an integrated toolset to enable best use of time and resources.
- The various functions involved in service operation may have overlapping or conflicting goals and activities. Roles and responsibilities must be defined in a way that ensures that these are all clearly understood.
- Designs for new services must include the operational requirements that need to be satisfied. Often, operations and development staff fail to engage and understand each other's needs.
- It must be clear what the operational requirements are, so that new services can be designed and implemented effectively and efficiently. Those designing a new service must understand up front what operational requirements need to be satisfied.

9   Related guidance

This chapter provides some information about other frameworks, best practices, models and quality systems that have synergy with the ITIL service lifecycle.

9.1   RISK ASSESSMENT AND MANAGEMENT

Risk may be defined as uncertainty of outcome, whether a positive opportunity or negative threat. Formal risk management enables better decision-making based on a sound understanding of risks and their likely impact.

A number of different methodologies, standards and frameworks have been developed for risk management. Each organization should determine the approach to risk management that is best suited to its needs and circumstances.

Approaches to risk management that should be considered include:

- Office of Government Commerce (2010). *Management of Risk: Guidance for Practitioners*. TSO, London.
- ISO 31000
- ISO/IEC 27001
- Risk IT[2]

9.2   ITIL GUIDANCE AND WEB SERVICES

ITIL is part of the Best Management Practice portfolio of best-practice guidance.

---

[2]   With the publication of COBIT 5, Risk IT will be included within COBIT.

The Best Management Practice website (www.best-management-practice.com) includes news, reviews, case studies and white papers on ITIL and all other Best Management Practice guidance.

The ITIL official website (www.itil-officialsite.com) contains reliable, up-to-date information on ITIL – including information on accreditation and the ITIL software scheme for the endorsement of ITIL-based tools.

Details of the core ITIL publications are:

- Cabinet Office (2011). *ITIL Service Strategy*. TSO, London.
- Cabinet Office (2011). *ITIL Service Design*. TSO, London.
- Cabinet Office (2011). *ITIL Service Transition*. TSO, London.
- Cabinet Office (2011). *ITIL Service Operation*. TSO, London.
- Cabinet Office (2011). *ITIL Continual Service Improvement*. TSO, London.

The full ITIL glossary, in English and other languages, can be accessed through the ITIL official site at:

www.itil-officialsite.com/InternationalActivities/
TranslatedGlossaries.aspx

The full range of ITIL-derived and complementary publications can be found in the publications library of the Best Management Practice website at:

www.best-management-practice.com/Publications-Library/IT-Service-Management-ITIL/

9.3 QUALITY MANAGEMENT SYSTEM

Quality management focuses on product/service quality as well as the quality assurance and control of processes. Total Quality

Management (TQM) is a methodology for managing continual improvement by using a quality management system.

ISO 9000:2005 describes the fundamentals of quality management systems that are applicable to all organizations which need to demonstrate their ability to consistently provide products that meet requirements. ISO 9001:2008 specifies generic requirements for a quality management system.

9.4   GOVERNANCE OF IT

ISO 9004 (Managing for the sustained success of an organization – a quality management approach) provides guidance on governance for the board and top management of an organization.

ISO/IEC 38500 is the standard for corporate governance of IT. The purpose of this standard is to promote effective, efficient and acceptable use of IT in all organizations.

9.5   COBIT

The Control OBjectives for Information and related Technology (COBIT) is a governance and control framework for IT management created by ISACA and the IT Governance Institute (ITGI).

COBIT is positioned at a high level, is driven by business requirements, covers the full range of IT activities, and concentrates on *what* should be achieved rather than *how* to achieve effective governance, management and control. ITIL provides an organization with best-practice guidance on *how* to manage and improve its processes to deliver high-quality, cost-effective IT services.

Further information about COBIT is available at www.isaca.org and www.itgi.org

9.6   ISO/IEC 20000 SERVICE MANAGEMENT SERIES

ISO/IEC 20000 is an internationally recognized standard for ITSM covering service providers who manage and deliver IT-enabled services to internal or external customers. ISO/IEC 20000-1 is aligned with other ISO management systems standards such as ISO 9001 and ISO/IEC 27001.

One of the most common routes for an organization to achieve the requirements of ISO/IEC 20000 is by adopting ITIL best practices.

Further details can be found at www.iso.org or www.isoiec20000certification.com

9.7   ENVIRONMENTAL MANAGEMENT AND GREEN/ SUSTAINABLE IT

'Green IT' refers to environmentally sustainable computing where the use and disposal of computers and printers are carried out in sustainable ways that do not have a negative impact on the environment.

The ISO 14001 series of standards for an environment management system is designed to assure internal and external stakeholders that the organization is an environmentally responsible organization.

Further details are available at www.iso.org

9.8   PROGRAMME AND PROJECT MANAGEMENT

The principles of programme management are key to delivering on time and within budget. Best management practice in this area is found in *Managing Successful Programmes* (MSP) (TSO, 2011).

Visit www.msp-officialsite.com for more information on MSP.

Portfolio, Programme and Project Offices (P3O) (TSO, 2008) is aimed at helping organizations to establish and maintain appropriate business support structures with proven roles and responsibilities.

Visit www.p3o-officialsite.com for more information on P3O.

Structured project management methods, such as PRINCE2 (PRojects IN Controlled Environments) (TSO, 2009) or the Project Management Body of Knowledge (PMBOK) developed by the Project Management Institute (PMI), can be used when improving IT services.

Visit www.prince-officialsite.com for more information on PRINCE2.

Visit www.pmi.org for more information on PMI and PMBOK.

9.9   SKILLS FRAMEWORK FOR THE INFORMATION AGE

The Skills Framework for the Information Age (SFIA) supports skills audit, planning future skill requirements, development programmes, standardization of job titles and functions, and resource allocation.

Visit www.sfia.org.uk for further details.

9.10 CARNEGIE MELLON: CMMI AND ESCM FRAMEWORK

The Capability Maturity Model Integration (CMMI) is a process improvement approach developed by the Software Engineering Institute (SEI) of Carnegie Mellon University. CMMI can be used to guide process improvement across a project, a division or an entire organization.

The eSourcing Capability Model for Service Providers (eSCM-SP) is a framework developed by ITSqc at Carnegie Mellon to improve the relationship between IT service providers and their customers.

For more information, see www.sei.cmu.edu/cmmi/

9.11 BALANCED SCORECARD

The balanced scorecard approach provides guidance for what companies should measure to provide a balanced view. The balanced scorecard suggests that the organization be viewed from four perspectives, and it is valuable to develop metrics, collect data and analyse the organization relative to each of these perspectives:

- The learning and growth perspective
- The business process perspective
- The customer perspective
- The financial perspective.

Further details are available through the balanced scorecard user community at www.scorecardsupport.com

9.12   SIX SIGMA

Six Sigma is a data-driven process improvement approach that supports continual improvement. The objective is to implement a measurement-oriented strategy focused on process improvement and defects reduction. A Six Sigma defect is defined as anything outside customer specifications.

There are two primary sub-methodologies within Six Sigma: DMAIC (Define, Measure, Analyse, Improve, Control) and DMADV (Define, Measure, Analyse, Design, Verify). DMAIC is an improvement method for existing processes for which performance does not meet expectations, or for which incremental improvements are desired. DMADV focuses on the creation of new processes.